WOMEN PIRATES
Eight Stories of Adventure

WOMEN PIRATES
Eight Stories of Adventure

Myra Weatherly

MORGAN
REYNOLDS
Incorporated

Greensboro

WOMEN PIRATES *Eight Stories of Adventure*

Copyright © 1998 by Myra Weatherly

Cover courtesy of
Delaware Art Museum
Howard Pyle, *An Attack on A Galleon,* 1905
From "The Fate of Treasure Town" by Howard Pyle
Oil on canvas

Photos courtesy of
The British Library London
Boston Public Library - Department of Rare Books and Manuscripts
National Maritime Museum—London

Library of Congress Cataloging-in-Publication Data
Weatherly, Myra.
  Women Pirates: eight stories of adventure / Myra Weatherly. — 1st ed.
  Includes bibliographical references and index.
  Summary: Recounts the life stories of eight notorious women pirates, including Grace
O'Malley, Anne Bonny, and Cheng I Sao.
    ISBN 1-883846-24-2
      1. Women Pirates—Juvenile literature [1. Women pirates. 2. Pirates.
3. Women—Biography] I. Title
G535. W4   1998
910.4'5'082—dc21

97-49407
CIP
AC

Printed in the United States of America
First Edition

Dedicated To
Jan

Contents

Introduction 9

Alfhild
Princess Pirate 12

Grace O'Malley
Irish Pirate Queen 21

Maria Cobham
"Dead Cats Don'tMew" 34

Mary Read
"Put Into Breeches" 45

Anne Bonny
"A Fierce and Couragious Temper" 57

Rachel Wall
Boston Pirate 73

Fanny Campbell
Revolutionary Pirate 84

Cheng I Sao
Chinese Pirate and Warlord 95

Bibliography 109

Index 111

A three-masted pirate lugger pursued by a British warship in the English Channel.

Introduction

With pitch and tar her hands were hard
Tho' once like velvet soft
She weighed the anchor, heav'd the lead
And boldly went aloft.

Author Unknown

Pirate! When you hear the word, you probably think of *men* roaming the high seas, searching for ships to plunder. Yet, there were *women* pirates.

They sailed, robbed, and fought. Some of the fiercest, cruelest, and most daring pirates who ever lived were women.

Piracy has existed since the earliest times. One account suggests the first water-borne snatch took place "in the far, dim ages when some naked savage, paddling himself across a tropical river met with another adventurer on a better tree trunk carrying a bigger bunch of bananas."

Homer's epic poems, written more than four thousand years ago, include references to piracy. Around 79 BC, Greek pirates seized a young Roman noble, Julius Caesar. He paid the pirates a large ransom for his release. Later, he captured and crucified his captors.

Alfhild is the first woman pirate to appear in the pages of history. Her father was a Scandinavian king in the fifth century. Although this story of a royal lady seeking adventure on the high seas has a legendary air about it, the characters were some of the early rulers of Denmark. During the Middle Ages, the Vikings—Scandinavian seafarers—in their dragon-headed ships plundered far afield, ravaging the coasts of Europe. Beginning in the 1200s, pirates and smugglers caused havoc to the southern shores of England.

In the sixteenth, seventeenth, and nineteenth centuries, pirates swarmed over all the oceans of the world, creating an age of exploitation and terror. An intensive period of piracy began in the Western world in the 1650s and ended around 1725. The last thirty-three years of this period of plundering on a massive scale earned the name—Golden Age of Piracy. The scene shifted to the Orient in the early nineteenth century as pirates scourged the China seas. An exceptional woman called Cheng I Sao commanded a fleet of 2,000 junks and 70,000 men and women. Surprising as it may seem, piracy flourishes in some parts of the world today.

From time immemorial, swashbuckling pirates have remained alive for us in stories, ballads, plays, and novels. Although based on myth, the fictional pirate expresses some of the genuine flavor of piracy.

In the panorama of the history of piracy, women are few. Stripped of the glamorized myths, the true story of women pirates emerges. Authenticated records tell tales of romance, brutality, and intrigue that are often far more compelling than fiction. Their names are not well known, but women pirates left their mark upon history.

Each of the stories presented here differs. Accounts of this bold, brutal breed of women have a common thread: each chose an adventurous, defiant lifestyle that broke out of old patterns and forged new molds.

Who they were, what they did, and how they did it continues to capture our imagination.

Alfhild
Princess Pirate

Alfhild, daughter of Gothic King Siward, was the first woman pirate to appear in the pages of history. The tale was already hundreds of years old when Saxo Grammacticus, medieval historian of Denmark, recorded her adventures in the twelfth century. Variations of the name Alfhild include "Alwilda" and "Alvilda."

Is the story true or is it a myth? No one can be sure because medieval historians often wove myth and history together, gleaning information from old songs, inscriptions, and tradition. However implausible the story may seem, certain aspects are based on fact: the characters were some of the early rulers of Denmark and piracy did exist in the Middle Ages in Scandinavia, what is now Denmark, Norway, and Sweden.

The well-recorded Viking raids began nearly four hundred years after the decline of the Roman Empire. In the preceding four centuries, not much that traveled by water had been worth plundering. Scholars have suggested overpopulation and famine as possible motives for the dramatic deluge of Scandinavian pirate attacks. Life was harsh, the soil unresponsive, and the weather unrelenting.

Whenever the fishing was not going well, these Norse pirates set out on long-distance pillaging and colonizing expeditions, navigating by sun, moon, and stars—often hidden behind massive cloud banks, making them unreliable guides. There were no maps, charts, lighthouses, compasses, or foghorns. Lack of instruments forced the Norsemen to hug the coast wherever possible. They were early masters of "island hopping."

The monasteries of Ireland, England, and France were treasure houses of gold and silver ornaments, jewels, and glittering brocades. They seemed to offer almost limitless prospects of loot to these northern pirates from a stark land.

A single shipload of spoils was enough to unleash an avalanche of greed that initiated centuries of wild and adventurous cold-blooded piracy. In Viking society, thievery was considered an honorable occupation and fighting reigned supreme. Children's games were actually lessons in warfare. Youngsters were trained to thrust a sword, to swing a battle-ax, and to throw a spear. Jumping, running, and wrestling took the place of reading, writing, and arithmetic. Skating, skiing, swimming, rowing, and horseback riding ensured the development of strong bodies.

These fearless and skilled raiders from the north carried out barbaric acts in the name of the Viking gods, their allies in any bloody fracas. Only by death in battle could a Norseman enter Valhalla, the warrior's heaven. To them, Christian and Muslim ideas of guilt and sin were meaningless.

Not only did the unrelenting and mobile sea rovers ransack wealthy targets, they invaded towns and villages on the coasts of Ireland, England, Scotland, France, Spain, North Africa, and Italy. They would row up the Thames or the Loire in their sleek, swift dragon ships like a swarm of dark red seabirds and prey on the countryside—stealing horses, burning, killing, looting—and vanish before anyone could take action.

The Norse marauders sailed down rivers to the Black Sea into what is now Russia, leaving a trail of plundered towns. Eventually, their brilliant striped sails appeared in Constantinople where the Byzantine emperor enrolled the towering fair-hairied pirates, with their insatiable addiction to drunkenness, gluttony, and brawls, as his bodyguards. They became the Varangers, a corps of regal gorillas, who terrified the empire as far afield as Alexandria and upper Egypt.

Saxo Grammacticus told the story of Alfhild against the backdrop of life in medieval times. In this seafaring area, there must have been women who answered the beckoning call of the sea. Saxo wanted to impress upon his readers that women pirates were real.

He wrote: "There were some women among the Danes who dressed themselves to look like men, and devoted almost every instant of their lives to the pursuit of war. For they abhorred all dainty living, and used to harden their minds and bodies with toil and endurance. They put away all the softness and lightmindedness of women, and inured their womanish spirit to masculine ruthlessness . . . They devoted those hands to the lance which they should rather have applied to the loom. They assailed men with their spears whom they could have melted with their looks, they thought of death and not of dalliance."

Alfhild's story provides an example of a royal lady seeking adventure on the high seas. Saxo's text gives no details of how she may have looked. The story implies that perhaps she was in her late teens or early twenties. Any seafarer in the North Sea would likely have had weathered, ruddy skin. Today's historians suggest that because Alfhild was a princess she would have worn ermine, black or white fox, sable or squirrel. She might have dined on broth, rye bread, cheese, whale, seal, or polar bear meat with beer or wine as a beverage. Her diet would also have included berries, apples, or hazelnuts. She may have walked with the rolling gait mariners develop to match the ship's movement.

An engraving made in the 1800s represents a nineteenth-century illustrator's perception of Alfhild. Her tall slim body and long sword as well as the warrior stance in the portrait indicate a strong, self-willed, and domineering woman.

Saxo's story tells that King Siward had two sons, Wemund and Osten, and a daughter, Alfhild, "who showed almost from her cradle such faithfulness to modesty, that she continually kept her face muffled in her robe ... Her father gave her "a viper and a snake to rear" to ensure her "close keeping." The historian explained: "For it would have been hard to pry into her chamber when it was barred by so dangerous a bolt."

Alf, son of King Sigar of Denmark, whose hair had such a "wonderful dazzling glow that his locks seemed to shine silvery," declared himself a wooer of Princess Alfhild. Siward's answer to Alf's appeal was "that he would accept that man for his daughter's husband of whom she made a free and decided choice." In Saxo's chronicles, Alfhild is not the only female allowed to choose or reject a suitor. Other women were being permitted to make their own decisions about suitors as well as women scorning the mates assigned to them.

Only Alfhild's mother was "stiff against the wooer's suit." She spoke to her daughter privately. Unmindful of her mother's warnings, the daughter "warmly praised her suitor for his valour..." Saxo also wrote that she was "captivated by charming looks."

Now the story takes a dramatic shift. Suddenly the demure, dutiful, and closeted princess is transformed. "Thus Alfhild was led to despise the young Dane; whereupon she exchanged woman's attire for man's attire, and no longer the most modest of maidens, began the life of a warlike rover." We are not told how her parents responded to this

This picture of Alfhild was drawn centuries after her death.

change in attitude or her desire to practice piracy — fighting and risking death. Saxo wrote: "In those days, trade and piracy went hand in hand." This acceptance of piracy may explain why no protest by her parents is recorded.

Having spurned her suitor, the princess recruited a crew of "many maidens who were of the same mind" and embarked on a career of sea roving. These like-minded maidens, attired as men, could have been her companions, or they may have come from the lower class of wandering women. In any case, they must have been a tough muscular bunch because the longboats relied more on oars than sails for propulsion. Fighting only with hand weapons required enormous physical strength and stamina.

Perhaps the women had learned their seafaring skills on fishing vessels in the absence of men and probably experienced killing by butchering farm animals, which was a common chore for medieval women.

After several expeditions, the women "happened to come to a spot where a band of rovers were lamenting the death of their captain who had been lost in war . . . " Apparently, the male pirates were so taken by the charm and agreeable manner of Alfhild that they asked her to join forces with them and be their "rover-captain." She agreed and "did deeds beyond the valour of woman." For months, the now co-ed pirate crew, under the command of Alfhild, plundered the Danish coast, terrorizing vessels.

Since subduing pirates was an important part of regal business, King Sigar sent the young crown prince of Denmark, Alfhild's rejected suitor, to conquer the treacherous robbers. Alf made "many toilsome voyages" in pursuit of the raiders. Finally, the Danes "crossed the frozen waters" and sailed to Finland. Upon entering a narrow gulf, they learned that the harbor was being held by a few ships.

Alfhild had already sailed her fleet into the same narrows. Seeing strange ships in the distance, the pirate captain, dressed for combat in armor and helmet, commanded her crew to row swiftly to meet them. The plan was to attack the foe before being attacked.

Alf's men tried to persuade him against attacking. But he ignored the logistics of sea warfare—a decision that later served him well.

A fierce sea battle occurred in the Gulf of Finland. Although Alfhild's pirates had been equal to the defenses of the poor coastal towns, they were no match for the well-trained royal navy. The sailors swarmed over the pirates, killing most of the crew. The Danes did not seem to wonder "whence their enemies got such grace of bodily beauty and such supple limbs."

When the battle began, Prince Alf "leapt on Alfhild's prow, and advanced toward the stern, slaughtering all that withstood him." His comrade, Borgar, ripped the helmet from the captain's head. Alf "seeing the smoothness of her chin, saw that he must fight with kisses and not with arms;

that the cruel spears must be put away, and the enemy handled with gentler dealings."

Standing before Alf was his adversary — "the woman whom he had sought over land and sea in the face of so many dangers. . ." Rejoicing that he had finally found Alfhild, he proposed marriage.

Alfhild accepted. Whether she was swept off her feet by Prince Alf's proposal directly to her instead of asking her father, or was persuaded by his bravery, we do not know.

Although Saxo's conclusion has the ring of a fairy-tale ending, Alf and Alfhild were married and had a daughter named Gurïd. Apparently, Alfhild changed "her man's apparel to a woman's," gave up her career, and retired from the sea.

Borgar, a member of the royal navy "wedded the attendant of Alfhild, Groa." Whatever happened to the other "maidens of the same mind," who survived the bloody battle, is not recorded in the chronicle. We can only speculate as to whether they carried on their ruthless and roving ways of living.

Years later, the Viking surge of piracy dwindled. Christianity was consolidated in Denmark around the year 1000, in Norway, fifty years later, and in Sweden almost one hundred years later. The end of the Viking era was followed by several centuries barren of much pirate activity.

Grace O'Malley
Irish Pirate Queen

Stories of notorious pirate Grace O'Malley, known in Ireland as "Granuaile," abound. Her sixteenth-century exploits spanned fifty years and extended from Scotland to Spain. Her history has gathered legends like barnacles. A tomb on Clare Island holds a skull reputed to be hers. Tradition states that a curse protects it from thieves.

Who was this "woman who overstepped the part of womanhood" and lives today somewhere in the fog of legend?

Grace O'Malley, "the great spoiler and chief commander and director of thieves and murderers at sea," lived in a remote region of Ireland for over seventy years. Official state dispatches from the age of Queen Elizabeth contain accounts of her deeds.

Grace O'Malley, the "Pirate Queen," belonged to a century of "exploration and discovery, of wars and intrigue, of armadas and invasions, of glorious empires at the pinnacle." Hers was the age of Henry VIII, Elizabeth I, Philip of Spain, Francis Drake, Walter Raleigh, and William Shakespeare.

Born in the early part of the sixteenth century, Grace was the only daughter of Dudara and Margaret O'Malley. Dudara (Black Oak) ruled Umhall, the country around island-strewn Clew Bay with its dangerous reefs and currents.

The daring, sea-going O'Malley clan differed from the majority of Irish clans in that the primary source of their income came from the sea. They sailed as far afield as Spain, Scotland, and Brittany in their agile galleys powered by oar and sail. They sold salted fish, beef hides, tallow, and woolens in lucrative markets abroad.

Records show that plundering by sea supplemented the O'Malleys' income. Details of their raids on the isolated bays and coves off the west coast of Ireland are a part of ancient histories.

In 1538, when Grace was about eight, the rumblings of English power drew closer to the western coast of Ireland. Until this time, the O'Malleys and their neighboring clans paid little attention to the affairs of the country. Independent chieftains ruled each state, spending their resources and energies on constant petty warfare and survival. Because of the O'Malleys' remote habitat, young Grace grew up in a period of relative freedom from outside powers.

Much of Grace's childhood is the subject of folklore. One legend tells of an incident in her early years on Clare Island.

A brood of eagles had been carrying off the O'Malleys' sheep, taking them to their nests high on a cliff. Grace decided to end this nuisance herself by climbing the cliff to the nest and slaughtering the birds. Supposedly, the talons of the angry eagles deeply gashed her forehead, leaving scars that never disappeared.

Grace's early childhood revolved around the family homes at Belclare and Clare Island. The O'Malleys, like other Irish families, also maintained monasteries. The abbey at Murrisk was near the O'Malleys home at Belclare. Around the outskirts of the O'Malleys' sphinx-like fortress nestled the thatched mud and stone cabins of his clan. In front stretched the sea. The clan's herds of cattle and sheep grazed on the hillsides.

Traveling bards entertained the chieftain's household in the winter. These poets and musicians also provided news and gossip from other parts of the country. Favorite pastimes included gambling and card playing "at which Grace clearly excelled."

In the summer, Grace's father moved his household to a "booley," a temporary summer dwelling in the uplands where the cattle herds could graze. These lacked the basic comforts of the permanent home. While "booleying," Dudara continued to fish and trade, unlike land-bound chieftains.

Grace's mother, Margaret, managed the household and served as hostess to the clan gatherings. Margaret supervised the work of the women—spinning, weaving and dyeing clothes, butter making, preparation of the meals, and upkeep of the residences.

Since the fifth century, when Christianity reached Ireland, a woman's place was in the home. Women's names appeared in historical records only if they were the wives of chieftains. From an early age, Grace's interests lay not in her mother's domain, but in her father's world of ships, trade, politics, and power.

Dudara O'Malley was a "swarthy, broad-shouldered chieftain, of great physical strength, his fair hair falling to his shoulders and cut in the traditional 'glib' or fringe across his forehead." He wore the chieftain's cloak, fastened with a gold pin and falling in folds to the ground. In his belt he carried a "Skeyne" or knife. He was a proud man who never submitted to the English crown.

Perhaps her father's character and even physical attributes caused Grace to emulate him, to dress like him, to adopt his lifestyle—and to become more like a son than a daughter. No doubt, her early years spent on the edge of the ocean instilled a love for the maritime that lasted throughout her life.

A legend explains Granuaile's nickname, "Grainne Mhaol" (Bald). As a young child, she pleaded to sail to Spain with her father. When her mother reminded Grace that a sailor's lot was no life for a young lady, Grace promptly cut off her long locks like the boys who sailed. Grace went to

Queen Elizabeth I ruled England during the years Grace O'Malley "overstepped the part of womanhood."

sea with her father, sailing to Spain and Portugal. She became an expert warrior on both land and sea.

At fifteen, Grace's father arranged for her to marry a local chieftain, Donal O'Flaherty, linking two of the most prominent seafaring families of western Ireland. She began her new life at Bunowen, her husband's tower-house fortress, located beside a concealed inlet.

Mystery shrouds much of Grace's life as the wife of the reckless and aggressive Donal. The marriage produced two sons and a daughter. In the beginning, Grace seemed to conform "to what her husband and society deemed a woman's role," assuming the duties as mistress of two castles.

Donal O'Flaherty, however, proved to be irresponsible, and his clansmen turned to his wife for help. Grace emerged as leader of the O'Flaherty clan. This began her life as a pirate.

Lumbering merchant ships on their way to Galway were prime targets for Grace and her men. Swooping out of cover of the islands in swift galleys, the pirates forced the ships to halt. Scrambling aboard, they pillaged and plundered. Laden with the loot, Grace and her men disappeared into the mists and safety of Bunowen.

Local officials were powerless against such attacks, and the English did not have the ships or sufficient knowledge of the country and its remote coastline to apprehend Granuaile. Clew Bay was unknown territory. Cartography was still being developed during the reign of Elizabeth.

Grace also took control of the clan's trading expeditions. She sailed to Munster, Scotland, Spain, and Portugal.

According to legend, Grace's husband died while trying to seize control of an island fortress known as Cock's Castle. After his death the Joyces, longtime enemies of the O'Flahertys, took the castle. With Donal dead, the Joyces were confident that the castle belonged to them. But the joy in the Joyces' camp ended abruptly when Grace led the O'Flahertys in a surprise attack and regained the castle.

Later, this island fortress was under siege again. Grace ordered her men to strip the lead roof off the castle and melt it down. The molten liquid spilled over the turrets onto the soldiers below, who quickly retreated to the mainland.

Although Grace proved to be a successful leader, Irish law did not allow a woman chieftain. Following the death of her husband, she returned to her father's domain on Clare Island, taking with her a band of two hundred men. She commanded the O'Malley fleets on errands of trade and piracy in what she described as "maintenance by land and sea"—earning both a fortune and a reputation as a fearless sea captain.

For over half a century, she led her men, contrary to the conventions of the time. Undoubtedly, her accomplishments contributed to her men's loyalty. "Outenduring and outdoing her men" she forged a lasting bond.

Grace was an expert at navigation and knew well the

dangerous coastline, her ships, and the elements of the wild Atlantic. Conditions on board ship in the sixteenth century were primitive. "Skin toughened under the barrage of wind and salt spray, hands and nails were hardened and split by hawser and canvas, bare feet became chafed from the rough swaying boards, sodden woolen trews and linen shirts itched, cold food lodged, undigested."

Eventually, international events affected Grace's maritime operations. Fearing Spain's use of Ireland as a back door to England, the English government, with its sheriffs, governors, and the military, pushed westward into remote areas such as Mayo. Realizing that she needed a more secure base for her ships and crews than Clare Island, Grace decided to remarry. She did the choosing this time, basing her decision on the castle rather than its owner.

Grace married Richard-in-Iron Bourke, who owned Rockfleet Castle on the north shore of Clew Bay. It was for "one year certain," and if after that period either party wished to withdraw, they were free to do so. One year later, Richard returned from one of his warring missions to find that Rockfleet Castle was locked against him. Grace shouted from the ramparts of the castle, "I dismiss you," meaning she was divorcing him. She informed him that his castle was now hers. But Grace and Richard eventually reunited and lived together at Rockfleet Castle.

Their son, Theobald, was born around 1567. Records show his name as Tibbot-na-Long, or "Theobald of the ships." According to stories surrounding his nickname, he was born on the high seas. The day after his birth, Turkish pirates attacked Grace's ship. As the battle raged on deck, her captain came below where Grace lay with her newborn son. He pleaded for help. She lambasted the captain: "May you be seven-times worse this day twelve months, who cannot do without me for one day." The new mother stormed onto the deck. The Turks, distracted by this disheveled female apparition, stood transfixed while Grace led her men to victory.

In 1576, Sir Henry Sidney, the first English deputy sent into western Ireland, met "the most feminine sea captain, Granny I Mallye." Why Grace risked capture by requesting a meeting with Sidney is open to speculation. Perhaps she realized that she could not survive without good relations with the English. Grace pledged loyalty to Sidney. But in so doing she gave her promise "a broad interpretation and continued as before, a scourge of the sea, taking tolls and raiding and pirating the ships that ventured within her domain."

Her husband, Richard, died in 1583 and Grace "gathered together all her own followers and with 1,000 head of cattle and mares became a dweller in Rockfleet." She was now fifty-three years old and seemed ready to carry on as before—but it was not to be.

As hostility between England and Spain intensified, the English governor of Ireland, Richard Bingham, tried to control the island nation. Eventually, he captured Grace and, as she later related to Queen Elizabeth, Bingham "caused a new pair of gallows to be made for her last funeral." But the chieftains of Mayo obtained her release by submitting hostages.

Bingham next took her son Tibbott-na-Long hostage in an attempt to ensure Grace's good behavior and confiscated her enormous cattle herds. Her oldest son, Owen O'Flaherty, died while in the custody of Bingham's brother, and her second son, Murrough, incurred his mother's anger by siding with Bingham. To punish Murrough, she "manned out her navy of galleys, landed in Ballinahinche where he dwelleth, burned his town and spoiled his people of their cattle and goods and murdered four of his men who made resistance." Then she sailed for Clew Bay, her galleys laden with the spoils of the attack.

In 1592, Grace suffered a blow to her power when Bingham seized part of her fleet. Time was running out, as even the outlying areas of Ireland came under the English net. A new map of the country depicting the remote havens of Ireland was issued. Grace's name appears on the map above the region that she ruled—the only woman so noted.

After Bingham imprisoned her son, Tibbott-na-Long for treason, Grace, in July of 1593 appealed directly to the queen of England, Elizabeth I. Aware that the queen knew of her piracy, Grace related her version of events and requested her son's release from prison.

Grace O'Malley met with Queen Elizabeth to negotiate the release of her son from an English prison.

Intrigued by the petition, the queen dispatched eighteen "articles of interrogatory"—or questions—to be answered by Grace. Her deft replies provide an informative account of her life. She followed her correspondence to court, sailing her ship from Clew Bay to London for an audience with Queen Elizabeth.

Unfortunately, details of the meeting of these two illustrious women are lost. The two rulers, both in their declining years, must have been a study in contrasts: one a weather-beaten woman in somber Gaelic dress; the other with chalk-like features in a richly embroidered gown sewn with jewels.

During the conversation with Elizabeth, a powdered and coiffed lady-in-waiting, noticing that Grace needed a handkerchief, presented a cambric and lace one to her. After using it, Grace tossed it into the fire. Elizabeth informed her that the handkerchief was meant to be kept in her pocket. An astonished Grace said that in Ireland they had a higher standard of cleanliness than to pocket a soiled article.

The "Pirate Queen" made such an impression on Elizabeth that she granted all of Grace's requests, going against the advice of Governor Richard Bingham. However, the queen underestimated the plotting talents of this "aged woman." Following her successful mission to London, Grace returned to her plundering ways, under the guise of fighting the queen's "quarrel with all the world." In 1597, at the age of 66, she sailed as far as Scotland, continuing her trade of "maintenance by land and sea."

Grace instilled in her son, Theobald, the art of survival so well that he sided with the English at Gaelic Ireland's last stand at the Battle of Kinsale in 1601, and was knighted in 1603.

Uncertainty shrouds the death of Grace O'Malley. Historians believe she died about 1603 and was buried in the abbey on Clare Island, at the edge of the ocean that sustained her long and eventful life. Rockfleet Castle still stands today, a sentinel overlooking the quiet waters of Clew Bay. In the west of Ireland, pirate Grace O'Malley's stone fortresses are reminders of a commanding woman, "famous for her stoutness of courage and person, and for sundry exploits done by her at sea."

Maria Cobham
"Dead Cats Don't Mew"

Early in the eighteenth century, Maria Cobham and her husband, Eric Cobham, followed a no-survivors policy. They held to an old pirate saying: "Dead cats don't mew."

Marie Lindsey was born in Plymouth, a bustling seaport in Devon, England. Plymouth was the home port of many famous adventurers. It was here in 1577 that Sir Francis Drake set out on his voyage around the world. In 1588, the English sailed from Plymouth to meet the enormous fleet of the Spanish Armada—so large that eyewitnesses said "the ocean groaned under its weight."

Records reveal little about Maria's early life. She grew up in Plymouth and dreamed of someday sailing on a voyage herself.

One day, as she walked down the main street, Maria noticed a dapper-looking sea captain. Dressed in fine clothes, he stood out in the throngs of sailors milling about the streets of Plymouth. After a few hours of conversation with Captain Eric Cobham in a quayside tavern, she went aboard his cutter. Maria listened as Cobham told how he had become a pirate.

Eric Cobham was born in Poole, Dorsetshire. At the age of eighteen, he joined a smuggling gang, running brandy from France to England. To celebrate his twenty-first birthday, he crossed into France with a band of smugglers and loaded ten thousand gallons of brandy aboard his sloop. He slipped back across the English Channel without being apprehended.

But a little later on, as he cruised across from France—with another heavy load of smuggled goods—an English cutter awaited him. The captured smugglers, including Cobham, spent two years in jail. Cobham told Maria that after his term at Newgate Prison, he joined a group of highwaymen. After a few months with the robbers, he abandoned them and traveled to Oxford and obtained a position as clerk at the Bradford House. The former smuggler found many opportunities to practice thievery in the hotel. One night, wandering around the hotel floors after midnight, he noticed a light under a third floor door. Peeking through a crack, Cobham discovered a man in the room counting a pile of gold.

Cobham, barely eking by on the few shillings paid him by the owner of the inn, decided to take action. Watching surreptitiously up and down the hall, he tapped on the door of the room. The lodger opened the door cautiously, but Cobham pushed him aside and grabbed for the bag of gold.

During the struggle that followed, Cobham drew his knife and killed the lodger. The murderer escaped with the gold. Later, he heard that the innkeeper had entered the same room—an hour after Cobham's crime—found the guest dead, and was wrongly accused of the murder. The wealthy lodger, Mr. Hayes, had come to Oxford to buy a substantial amount of property. The innkeeper knew of the gold and had made plans to murder Hayes.

Following two weeks at Newgate Prison, the unfortunate innkeeper swung from the gallows for a crime he intended to commit but did not.

With four hundred pounds of gold, Cobham bought a new cutter at Bridgeport and mounted her with fourteen guns. He had no trouble recruiting a crew from the docks. In eighteenth century Britain, homeless families roamed the streets, and scrawny orphans begged on every corner. Many were glad to take up the life of a pirate. English rulers issued threats, bribes, and proclamations to end piracy, but with little success.

On his first cruise as a pirate, Cobham set off to plunder the North Sea. He soon sighted a ship from East India heading up the channel toward Bristol. He captured the vessel.

After overcoming the crew, the pirates forced the captain to reveal the whereabouts of his wealth. Cobham explained to Maria how he had persuaded the frightened captain to turn over his treasure, no less than forty thousand pounds

Sir Francis Drake, who earned the respect of his country as a pirate, set sail from Maria's hometown, the port city of Plymouth, to begin his round the world voyage.

in gold sovereigns, intended for the purchase of Chinese opium. Then, with this hoard in his possession, Cobham thrust his rapier through the captain's heart, sewed him up in a sack and, with rocks for ballast, dumped the body overboard.

Cobham instructed his pirates to carry out the same procedure with the other members of the captured crew. Maria listened, enchanted as Cobham described the scene: the terrible screams, yells of battle-crazed pirates, shrieks of the wounded. The deck was soon awash with blood. It took until midnight to complete the massacre. Then they stuffed the bodies in bags filled with rocks and tossed them overboard.

Having no use for the ship, the young captain scuttled the vessel. As he watched the beautiful ship disappear into the deep, he relished his extraordinary luck. Then he sailed into Plymouth harbor where he met Maria.

Young Maria Lindsey, who apparently came of good parentage, was not in the least disturbed by Cobham's cruelty. His adventures so captivated her that she decided to spend her life with him. The following day, she married Captain Cobham and set off on her honeymoon on a fourteen-gun cutter. Soon, more luckless sailors would be at the bottom of the ocean in canvas bags.

At first, having Maria on board caused some murmuring among the crew because they were not allowed to have women on their voyages. But Maria soon won the allegiance of the crew by using her influence with the captain to lighten their punishment when he was disciplining them.

Maria was an apt pupil. She soon became as vicious a pirate as her husband, capturing and scuttling ship after ship.

When the pirates captured a craft with a young naval officer aboard, Maria liked his uniform so much that she had him stripped of his clothes in front of the other pirates. Then she ran him through with her sword. Shoving his body into a sack, she sewed him up and heaved him overboard. Maria wore the dead man's uniform from then on. She liked the outfit so much that she had replicas made and wore them both at sea and in port.

One day, while roaming the high seas, these daring sea bandits narrowly escaped capture by a British man-of-war. Fearing that Captain Cobham had been recognized, Maria suggested that they sail across the Atlantic to the New England coast. A month later, they sighted land—Nantucket Island.

The pirates went ashore at No Man's Land and liked it so much that they decided to spend the summer. Cobham, supposedly, buried fifteen thousand golden guineas on the island.

Later, after pillaging at Block Island, Cobham and his crew sailed for northern waters. There they lay in wait for vessels passing between Cape Breton and Prince Edward

Island on route to Quebec from London. The pirates took money and merchandise from the captured vessels, killing the crews in the usual manner and scuttling the ships.

Maria always took an active part in the skirmishes. One day, using a recently stolen little dirk, she stabbed the captain of a Liverpool brig through the heart. Murder for her was a pleasure and a sport.

On another occasion, to indulge a whim, she insisted that a captain and his two mates be tied to a windlass. Then Maria went below. She came back on deck, brandishing eight pistols. From a distance of twenty feet, she fired gun after gun until the last spark of life in the three men vanished. According to tradition, she never missed a shot.

For twenty years, the Cobhams sailed the high seas and amassed a fortune they hid in several English banks and buried on many of the Atlantic islands. Finally, Captain Cobham grew weary of butchery and scuttling ships. He wanted to settle down. Maria did not. She finally agreed with the condition that Cobham would buy Mapleton Hall, an elegant estate in Dorset, her husband's homeport.

While Cobham went ashore to arrange for the purchase, Maria, for reasons unknown, took the crew out by herself. The next day, she overtook an East India merchant ship off Scotland. After a fierce encounter, she captured the vessel.

Taking the survivors aboard the cutter, Maria ordered the crew to put them in irons on the deck. Then she went into the galley and made poisoned stew. Within an hour of eating

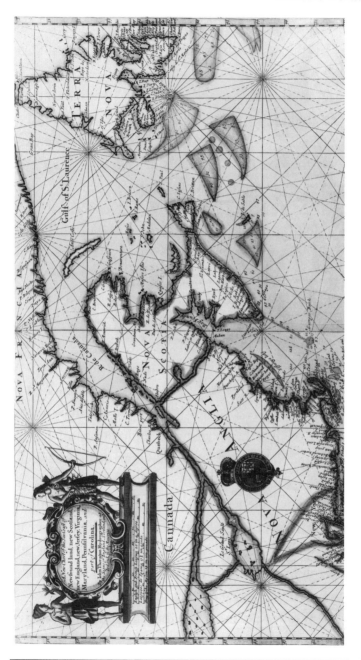

Maria and Eric Cobham sailed the north Atlantic, and hid stolen loot on islands off the coast of North America.

the stew, all the prisoners were dead. Maria disposed of the bodies by throwing them overboard—no sacks and no sewing up this time.

She returned to Dorset and learned that her husband had not been able to buy the mansion at Mapleton after all. A short time later, Cobham did buy a large estate near Le Harve on the coast of France. It had its own snug little harbor. Here the retired pirates kept a pleasure yacht, employing some of the former crew as officers and sailors. Maria still wore her naval uniform and went on fishing expeditions.

The Cobhams began to raise a family. Within five years, they had two sons and a daughter, and Maria and her husband had given up piracy—almost.

One day, while on a pleasure cruise, they encountered a big West Indian brig that lay becalmed just outside the bay. The couple decided to pay a social call on the captain of the merchant ship. Aboard the brig, they were enjoying the hospitality of their host when the temptations of former years became too strong. It took no more than eye contact between the couple to put a fiendish plan into action.

Maria invited the captain to board her yacht. Cobham whipped out a pistol and shot the captain through the head. Then they subdued the crew of the merchantman and disposed of the corpses in the usual manner by sewing them up in gunnysacks and throwing them overboard.

Cobham sailed the prize into the harbor on his property.

After altering the name of the brig, Maria and her husband took her to Bordeaux. They were able to sell her for a good price—no questions asked, still adding more to their riches. This deed turned out to be the last act of piracy for the Cobhams. They returned to the quiet of their estate.

Not long after, the Duc de Chartres visited Cobham and proposed that the ex-pirate take over the judgeship of the county courts. The magistrate had just died, and they were looking for an honest, reputable citizen to replace him. Stunned by the offer, Cobham wanted to decline, but Maria insisted that he accept. The aging pirate was now a judge! He found himself overseeing hundreds of cases for the next twelve years. Ironically, this couple of blackguards not only escaped punishment for their crimes but also gained respectability. Judge Cobham became famous for his fairness and condemnation of wrongdoing!

However, Maria did not adjust well to retirement. Possibly haunted by the specters of her grim past, she began to grow despondent. One day she told her husband that she needed some time alone to think. She went for a long walk along the towering cliffs and never returned.

Her husband found her cloak and scarf at the edge of a precipice. Two days later her body washed ashore. This came as no surprise to her husband because he had discovered an empty laudanum bottle with her cloak and scarf at the top of the cliff. Laudanum had been Maria's favorite poison.

Maria's suicide left Judge Eric Cobham conscious stricken. Although he never showed the slightest remorse before, he was now obsessed by the memory of the terrible deeds he had committed during his long period of crime at sea. He spent long hours at the local church in conference with the pastor.

Cobham lived to a ripe old age. Before he died, he called in the minister for his last confession. He revealed that, during the last twelve years, he had laboriously written out all the crimes that he and Maria committed in their many years of piracy. He made the pastor promise to publish the detailed confession after his death.

The published confession was an embarrassment to Cobham's socially prominent children and grandchildren. The descendants would have preferred to have the adventures of their wicked ancestors buried with them. Despite the family's efforts to buy the books up as rapidly as they appeared to keep them off the market, the story of Maria Cobham, woman pirate of iniquity, survived.

Mary Read
"Put Into Breeches"

"Milord, we plead our bellies."

On Monday, November 28, 1720, in a jam-packed Jamaican courtroom, spectators erupted with laughter as the two shackled pirates made their plea. The prisoners were not joking. They were indeed pregnant. In the eighteenth century, expectant mothers—no matter how guilty—escaped the hangman's noose because the law did not allow an unborn child to be killed.

One of the condemned women was Mary Read. She sailed the Caribbean beneath the black flag during the "Golden Age of Piracy"—the era of the greatest outburst of piracy the world has ever known.

Published four years after the trial, a history of the "pyrates" includes the exploits of Mary Read and Anne Bonny, the only known women pirates of the "Golden Age." The author of the 1724 bestseller, *The General History of the Robberies and Murders of the Most Notorious Pyrates,* was a mysterious Captain Charles Johnson. The historian used trial transcripts, contemporary newspaper reports, and "living witnesses to justify what we have laid down, including some particulars which were not so publicly known." According to one description, the story is "as strange a blend of fact and fiction . . . ever concocted." The author, anticipating this kind of reaction, acknowledged in the preface to the *History* that "it might be thought the story was no better than a novel or romance."

Mary Read's route to the Caribbean began in England. Her "young and airy" mother was pregnant when her sailor husband went to sea and never returned. In due time, she gave birth to a son.

Soon after, she discovered she was expecting a second child. Taking her infant son and her "secret," she left the urban squalor of London to live in the country where a tragedy not uncommon to the era struck. The baby boy became ill and died. Mary, the illegitimate daughter, was born a few months later, near the end of the seventeenth century.

Life was harsh for a single woman with an illegitimate child. For four years the small family struggled to survive in the country. Finally, at her wit's end, Mrs. Read trudged back to London, hoping to receive help from her deceased husband's mother. She decided the best way to get this help was to pass Mary off as her dead half-brother. Mrs. Read had never reported her son's death or Mary's birth to the relatives. She trained Mary to talk and act like a boy and

Mary Read learned how to fight like a man while serving as a soldier in the War of Spanish Succession.

exchanged her daughter's dress for a boy's breeches and coat. If she could make the grandmother think Mary was her grandson, their reception would be much warmer.

The scheme worked, almost too well. The grandmother offered to let the "lad" and his mother live with her. Sensing the risks of such an arrangement, Mrs. Read declined, but accepted a weekly allowance for their support. For many years, Mary maintained her false identity to keep the allowance.

Mary was thirteen when her grandmother died. The allowance stopped. The Reads were penniless again.

Mrs. Read solved the problem this time by hiring Mary—dressed in boy's attire—out as a footboy to a French lady. Mary did not object to dressing as a boy. Being a boy gave her more freedom at a time when girls led extremely sheltered lives

But Mary's nature demanded more excitement than the dullness of blacking boots for a living. "Growing bold and strong, and having also a roving mind," she enlisted as a cabin boy on board a British warship. It was possible to get away with such a fraud since recruits had no medical examinations in the 1700s. Servicemen seldom bathed or washed the entire body. They habitually slept in their clothes. To pass as a man, a woman needed only to bind her upper body with a sash before donning a uniform.

Mary found the routine life of a seaman in the Royal Navy boring. After a short stint, she deserted and crossed the English Channel to Flanders (now Belgium and part of France). She joined a regiment of Flemish foot soldiers and served as a cadet in the War of the Spanish Succession. "She behaved herself with a great deal of Bravery" during the long marches, artillery barrages, and bayonet charges. Mary was fearless, daring, and ambitious. She hoped to earn a commission as an officer, but soon discovered that poor people did not rise through the ranks. Promotions were bought and sold.

Disappointed, she transferred to a cavalry regiment. She loved riding into battle and won "the esteem of all her Officers." No one suspected that she was a girl.

One day a new man joined the troop and was assigned to her tent. When Mary saw this handsome, strapping young soldier, she fell in love. Strange new emotions stirred within her as she galloped beside him in battle. She was in love with a man who didn't even know she was a woman. She became absentminded and neglected her military duties. Mary insisted on accompanying her bunkmate wherever he went. Her odd behavior convinced her companions that Trooper Read had lost "his" mind.

Unable to contain her feelings any longer, Mary blurted out her secret. Astounded at first, the soldier soon returned her love and asked her to marry him.

At the close of the campaign, Mary married her former tent mate to the delight of her comrades. The regiment paid for the wedding, including the bride's trousseau. For the first time in her life, Mary dressed as a woman—probably wearing fancy shoes, petticoats, and a low-cut silk dress.

"Two troopers, marrying each other, made a great noise." They could not stay in the army and received honorable discharges. With contributions from the regiment, they opened The Three Horseshoes tavern, near Breda in Holland. Uniformed servicemen crowded the tavern every night. Mary seemed content in her role as a woman.

Like her mother, Mary was destined for a short married life. Her beloved husband died suddenly, bringing to an end the only domestic interlude in her life. Then she suffered a second blow—the return of peace that took away her English military customers. Brokenhearted, the impoverished widow gave up the empty inn, and her dress, for good.

Remembering the smell of gunpowder and the shouts of charging soldiers, Mary Read "again assumed her man's apparel." She enlisted in an infantry regiment in Holland. But life in a peacetime garrison was far too dull for her. She left the army and signed on a Dutch merchantman bound for the Caribbean, hoping to find excitement in the New World—a decision that assured a name for her in history.

The island-studded Caribbean, with scalloped shores of countless inlets and cays, was the focus of intense pirate activity from 1492 until the nineteenth century. No ship was safe. Settlements along the Spanish Main (Spanish possessions along the coasts of Central and South America) did not escape the plundering.

During the centuries following Christopher Columbus, European nations jockeyed for control of the New World and its riches. The powers of Europe pitted their expansionist forces against one another as wars waged over the islands of the West Indies and the Spanish Main.

Pirates of every nationality, color, and creed preyed on silver and gold laden galleons, merchant ships, and slavers. Despite the religious antagonisms and reversal of alliances that divided their countrymen, pirate crews varied in their ethnic and religious makeup. Multicultural seafarers played leading roles in the geopolitical drama, lasting three centuries.

Today, the term buccaneer is used loosely to refer to lawless adventurers on the high seas. The word originated from their custom of smoking meat on *boucans*—a French word for the wooden grills. The buccaneers, with a burning hatred for anything Spanish, lived off the land with the sky as their roof. They graduated from "cowkillers" to sea robbers, swooping out from the many narrow channels and creeks to prey upon unsuspecting merchant ships.

Buccaneers plundered Caribbean and Spanish coastal settlements during the seventeenth century. The original buccaneers were French political and religious refugees who roamed the island of Hispaniola that is now Haiti and the Dominican Republic. The New World's mineral wealth also attracted Protestant Dutch *Zee Rovers*. The English called them *freebooters*. The Spanish government regarded foreign seamen as *piratas*, hated interlopers.

For thirty-three years during the Golden Age of Piracy—between 1692 and 1725—pirate raiders terrorized the sea-lanes and disrupted trade. They ran their vessels as the buccaneers had done before them, electing their own captains and signing a set of articles, or rules, before setting sail.

By the late 1690s, British colonies along the Atlantic coast from Massachusetts to the Carolinas welcomed the sea rovers in protest of the English monopoly on manufactured goods, as well as unfair prices. All the leading colonial seaports—New York, Boston, Philadelphia, Charleston—did business with the pirates.

Rebellious seafarers of that era signed aboard pirate vessels, lured by stories of vast treasures taken in forays. Often, the life of a pirate was chosen for reasons other than mere lust for wealth. Many sailors turned outlaw to live a life of freedom. They wanted to escape an oppressive caste system that permitted liberty only to the wealthy and well born. This was what Mary Read hoped to do.

Before reaching the Caribbean, the Dutch vessel on which Mary sailed came under attack by English pirates from New Providence, a Bahamian haven for pirates. This was Mary Read's first encounter with pirates. The pirate captain forced Mary, the only "Englishman" on board, to join the marauders. After plundering the vessel, the pirates allowed the ship to continue on her journey.

Mary, eager to live life to its fullest, did not hesitate when

The original buccaneers were French refugees who hated the Spanish and preyed on the growing trade with the New World.

the captain growled for her to make her mark and join the pirates. By signing the ship's articles," she agreed to go "on the account," as the eighteenth-century pirates called it—meaning "No Prey, No Pay."

For a time, she sailed with the pirates, seeing plenty of action and expertly wielding her cutlass and pistol. Life aboard a pirate ship meant moments of intense excitement and terrifying danger when seizing a prize. After capturing a prize, the pirates beached their ship in a secluded bay or cove to divide the treasure and celebrate.

A favorite pastime of the pirates was to hold a mock trial with buffoonish ceremony. Each pirate had a chance to play judge and prisoner. Music played an important part, particularly songs sung in rhythm to work—chanteys and bawdy ballads, accompanied by fiddles, oboes, and recorders.

As a member of the pirate crew, Mary would have been expected to help with the repairing of spars, sails, rigging, and careening. At regular intervals, it was necessary to careen the ship in order to maintain speed and maneuverability. Careening involved tilting the ship to one side and scraping off the weed and shell-encrusted bottom, and putting on a form of anti-fouling layer.

She likely went in search of food and fresh water to restock the ship. The erratic diet of pirates included sea turtles, goats, monkeys, and snakes, some of which they salted for future use. Europeans disliked the vegetables in use by the natives of the West Indian islands.

One of the ways the pirates ridiculed the laws they defied was by having mock trials, with pirates playing judge and prisoner.

Mariners preferred beer or wine since water on board ship quickly became undrinkable. They seldom used forks. Most pirates ate with their fingers. One source describes their table manners: "They eat in a very disorderly manner more like a kennel of hounds. . ." Meals were eaten in the cramped sleeping quarters, engulfed by the smell of food, vermin, and excess cargo.

"After following this Trade for some Time," Mary and her shipmates accepted the royal pardon in 1718 offered by Woodes Roger, governor of the Bahamas. The record shows that the entire company voluntarily surrendered and lived quietly ashore, "with the fruits of their adventures," on an island some distance from New Providence.

Mary soon missed the free-roving ways of a pirate. When her money ran out, she packed her gear and headed back to sea. Along with several other ex-pirates, she went to New Providence and enlisted aboard a privateer, an armed vessel licensed to attack and seize the vessels of an enemy nation. Mary had government approval to sail against the Spaniards.

As soon as the ship left dock and New Providence disappeared below the blue horizon, the crew mutinied, took control of the vessel, and ran up the black flag. This mutiny began Mary's association with Jack Rackam and Anne Bonny. She never left pirating again.

Anne Bonny
"A Fierce and Couragious Temper"

The other woman on trial that balmy day in November 1720 was Anne Bonny. The judge, Sir Nicholas Lawes, his floppy gray judicial wig askew, pronounced Anne Bonny, partner of Mary Read, an outlaw "confirmed in all wicked practices—a lusting, thieving, oathing female, best made use of on the gallows." The mob listening outside the Admiralty Court at St Jago de la Vega, Jamaica, jeered.

This was not Anne's first trial. Before turning pirate, Anne had appeared in court. Her spectacular beauty saved her on that occasion. Jamaican court records show that the judge declared: "A more delectable doxie I have never seen—nor, for that matter, a more brazen one." She received a light sentence: threat of a flogging, if she did not behave.

Like Mary Read, Anne Bonny was "put into Breeches" at an early age because of a complicated family situation. She was born in Cork, Ireland, about 1700. Anne was the illegitimate child of a prominent lawyer, William Cormac, and Peg Brennan, the family maid. The lawyer's wife had left him because of his "dissolute way of life."

The scandal hurt Cormac's law practice. He decided to leave Ireland forever and start a new life in North America. Taking his mistress and their child, he settled in Charleston, South Carolina—a booming seaport then known as Charles Towne.

Cormac prospered in the new land. Not only was he in great demand as an attorney, he engaged in trading and became a wealthy plantation owner. Daughter Anne, now wearing appropriate clothes, developed into a spunky, strong-willed young woman, with her own room, her own horses, her own dogs, and much of the time her own way. She dressed in the finest materials and received an education from the best tutors.

Anne was about fifteen when her mother died. The young girl with "a fierce and couragious Temper" took over her father's household. She soon earned a fearsome reputation when, during a fit of passion that matched her flaming red hair, she killed a serving girl with a knife. She allegedly responded to the advances of a suitor by attacking him with such ferocity that he remained bedridden for several weeks.

Anne accompanied her father on trading trips to water-front offices, warehouses, and the teeming docks of Charleston. Bawdy songs and shouts wafted through the air from the rowdy waterfront taverns. Pirate ships brought in much of the merchandise: cotton, sugar, spices, indigo, dyewoods, and silks. Her father probably did business with pirates.

From an early age, Anne Bonny was known as a girl with a "fierce and couragious Temper."

Despite her growing reputation as a spitfire, Anne had many suitors. She spurned them all and married, without informing her father, a penniless seaman named James Bonny.

With his plans for marrying Anne to a prosperous Carolina merchant dashed, Cormac "turned her out of Doors." James Bonny, disappointed in seeing a fortune escape him, whisked his bride off to the pirates' nest on the island of New Providence in the Bahamas.

In the early eighteenth century, the stench from Nassau— roasting meat, smoke, unwashed bodies, defecation, and rotting garbage stewing together under the broiling sun— filled the air, long before the island came into view. Pirate sloops and captured merchant ships crowded the shimmering blue waters of the harbor. Abandoned prizes lay rotting on the beach; their ribs stripped as bare as skeletons. Ragged and dirty tents, improvised from discarded sails, fluttered in the trade winds like hundreds of unmade beds. In disordered array, shacks of driftwood thatched with palm fronds littered the edge of the woods. The forest rustled and the water lapped against the wharves, in and out of tiny caves along the beach.

Life in the zany shantytown was chaotic. Slovenly women screamed at one another as they prepared food around open campfires. They screeched at youngsters who toddled amid the filth. Babies cried. Dogs yelped. Parrots shrieked obscenities. Singing and shouting echoed along the waterfront. Pirates stumbled from tavern to tavern day and night.

Soon after Anne and her sailor husband arrived at this pirate enclave, she lost interest in Bonny. She reacted with disgust when he turned informer for Governor Woodes Rogers, who was commissioned by the British government to stamp out piracy. She began looking elsewhere for companionship.

The rich silks and golden trinkets in the market dazzled Anne, as did the bronze-faced, bearded pirates along the waterfront. Anne frequented the harbor side taverns, often seeking the company of swashbuckling pirate captains such as Charles Vane, Blackbeard, and Ben Hornigold.

Then she met the bold and reckless Captain John Rackam. His fondness for splashy waistcoats, bright ribbons, and gaudy calico breeches earned him the nickname "Calico Jack." Rackam came into Nassau to claim the king's pardon and to receive a privateering commission. The dashing pirate captain was the answer to Anne's unfilled yearning for a life at sea.

Calico Jack lavished Anne with flashy baubles from his booty. He even tried to buy her from her husband. Divorce by sale was an accepted practice at that time. But James Bonny refused. He complained to Governor Rogers, who ordered Anne to return to her husband. Instead, Anne ran away with Rackam.

That Rackam had no ship at this time only added to the

bold adventure. Anne slipped aboard a sloop anchored in Nassau harbor and gathered information while Calico Jack rounded up a handful of his old cronies. On a rainy night, the gang swarmed over the gunwales of the vessel with Anne in the lead. Wearing an ordinary seaman's garb, carrying a sword in one hand and a pistol in the other, Anne surprised the two men on watch. She whispered to them that she would blow out their brains if they resisted. They did not resist.

The pirates cast off from the ship's moorings in the dark of night. The sloop glided silently out of the harbor. Down came the British flag. Up went the black flag. Anne Bonny and Calico Jack Rackam sailed off into the blue waters of the Bahamas and onto the pages of history.

The pirates cruised the Caribbean, taking and pillaging a number of small prizes, and even raiding some shore installations. Anne, dressed in men's clothing and wielding a cutlass with the best of the crew, fought and plundered brutally. Her ruthlessness infected her most personal life. Once, she went ashore in Cuba to have a baby. After the delivery, she abandoned the child to rejoin Rackam.

A year later, the king ordered a new amnesty. Calico Jack decided to take this one. He went to New Providence and took the pardon, promising never to resort to piracy again. He signed aboard a legal privateer. Anne, disguised as a man, accompanied him. Only a few days out of port, the crew mutinied. Rackam and Anne were the ringleaders.

Captain Jack Rackam's fondness for fancy clothes earned him the nickname "Calico Jack."

Aboard the privateer turned pirate was a handsome, clean-cut young man who caught the roving eye of Anne Bonny. Anne admired the sailor's skill and daring. The shipboard friendship became a strong attraction, especially for Anne. She decided to reveal her identity, only to discover that the object of her desire was hiding the same secret. "He" was not a man, but Englishwoman Mary Read, who passed as an ordinary sailor. Both agreed to keep each other's secret.

In the weeks that followed, Anne Bonny and Mary Read fought side by side. One writer wrote that "None among Rackam's crew were more resolute or ready to Board or undertake any Thing that was hazardous as Mary Read and Anne Bonny."

Calico Jack, disturbed by Anne's interest in the young sailor, threatened to cut his "rival's" throat. To dispel Rackam's jealous rage, Mary let him in on the secret.

For some months, Rackam and his crew cruised the Caribbean, taking and looting merchant ships homeward bound from Jamaica. Forced to join the pirates in one of these successful raids was a handsome navigator, with engaging manners. "At least, he was so in the eyes of Mary Read."

Mary fell in love with the young captive. She wasted no time in telling him that she was a woman. He returned her love, promising they would wed at the end of the voyage. Mary agreed to what she later termed "as good a marriage in conscience as if it had been done by a minister in a church."

During the cruise, Mary demonstrated her affection in one of the "most generous Actions that ever Love inspired." Following a quarrel with a hulking brute of a pirate, Mary's "husband" was challenged to a duel. Fearing that the navigator—who was not an experienced fighter—would be killed, Mary deliberately provoked an argument with the same man. She challenged him to a duel two hours before the already scheduled duel.

Dueling was the accepted manner of settling disputes among pirates and conformed to a distinctive code. The participants went ashore to battle with cutlass and pistol until there was only one survivor.

Mary and her opponent both missed on the exchange of pistol shots. A long and bloody contest with cutlasses followed. The duel ended with Mary running the man through, wounding him mortally. Just as the ruffian crumpled in the sand, the navigator arrived for his scheduled duel—to find Mary standing over the dead pirate. An account of this incident came out at the trial.

By midsummer of 1720, Nassau was no longer a base for the outlaw nation. British forts defended the land. Ex-pirates, who now sailed under the British flag, protected the sea. Most of the pirates of the West Indies abandoned their old haunts. Only a few diehard brigands continued to follow the sweet trade in the Caribbean. One of that dwindling

Mary Read hurried to kill a man who had challenged her lover to a duel

number was Calico Jack and his crew, including Mary Read and Anne Bonny. But their days were numbered.

In late September, Rackam and his crew paid a call at Harbor Island. They captured fishing vessels, taking provisions, and gear. Then they landed on Hispaniola, where they slaughtered cattle to replenish their supplies.

By October, Rackam was operating off the north coast of Jamaica. He captured a schooner and one or two small trading vessels. Coasting the island in this manner proved to be Calico Jack's downfall.

Word reached the governor of Jamaica in November 1720 that Rackam lay anchored just off Negril Point on the

Mary Read exposes her breast to a man she has fatally wounded in a duel. The legend of the fierce women pirates Anne Bonny and Mary Read began soon after their deaths.

western end of Jamaica. Bounty hunter Captain Jonathan Barnet set sail in a heavily armored privateer, hoping to capture the unrelenting pirate.

The navy sloop surprised the tipsy pirates at ten o'clock at night. Rackam's big guns boomed. Captain Barnet's men fired across the narrow space of water between the two ships and threw grappling hooks over her gunwales, lashing the two vessels together. Sailors stormed aboard.

In the skirmish, all the pirates, including the once daring Captain Rackam, fled below deck—except for Anne Bonny, Mary Read, and one of the crew. They remained topside to defend the ship. Howling like banshees, the two women flew at the sailors, firing their pistols and swinging their cutlasses.

Mary drew two loaded pistols and screamed at the cowards below deck to "come up and fight like men." There was no answer. Realizing all was lost, she raised the hatch cover and turned both of her pistols into the hold. She pulled the triggers, killing one of the cowering pirates and wounding several others.

A moment later, the women, outnumbered, lost the battle.

The sailors slapped the surviving pirates in chains and took them to St. Jago de la Vega, (now Spanish Town) Jamaica to stand trial. After a brief imprisonment, they came before the Admiralty Court. Most of the men were tried on Wednesday, November 16, 1720. At the trial, Mary Read's young lover and several others claimed they served as pirates against their wills. They were set free.

Charles Johnson's book on the pirates includes a frequently quoted statement that is absent from the court transcript. Mary, when asked why she would risk public execution for the sake of pirating, replied: "That to hanging, she thought it no great hardship, for, were it not for that, every cowardly fellow would turn Pirate, and so infest the seas that men of courage must starve; that if it was put to the choice of the pirates, they would not have the punishment less than death, the fear of which kept some dastardly rogues honest; and that . . . the ocean would be crowded with rogues, like the land, and no merchant would venture out; so that the trade in a little time would not be worth following."

The writer Johnson claims that Mary commended the court for having acquitted her "husband." and stated that "they had both resolved to leave the Pirates the first opportunity and apply themselves to some honest livelihood."

Calico Jack Rackam and eight of his pirates were found guilty and sentenced to be hanged. By "special Favour," Rackam saw Anne before his execution. The visit brought him little consolation. The heavy iron door to Anne's cell creaked open. The once dashing figure, now a manacled man, shuffled into the cell. Anne's parting words stunned Calico Jack. She told him that she was "sorry to see him there, but if he had fought like a Man, he need not have been hang'd like a Dog."

Calico Jack, his leg irons clanking on the stone floor, stumbled outside. The waiting guards led him to the scaffold and the hangman's rope. On Friday, November 18, 1720, Captain John Rackam was hanged at Gallows Point at Port Royal. Afterward, his body was put into an iron cage and hung from a gibbet on Deadman's Cay "for a publick Example and to terrify others from such-like evil Practices." Today the small island is called Rackam's Cay.

A week later, Anne Bonny, not yet twenty years old, and Mary Read were tried on the same charges. Additional witnesses testified in the women's trial. Dorothy Thomas, who was in a canoe when the pirates attacked her, gave the following description: "The two women prisoners . . . wore men's jackets, and long trousers, and handkerchiefs tied about their heads; and that each of them had a machet and pistol in their hands, and cursed and swore at the men, to murder the deponent . . . and the deponent further said, that the reason of her knowing and believing them to be women then was by the largeness of their breasts."

Thomas Dillon testified that "Anne Bonny, one of the prisoners at the bar, had a gun in her hand, and they were both very profligate, cursing and swearing much, and very ready and willing to do anything on board."

Found guilty of the charges, Anne Bonny and Mary Read received death sentences. After informing the court that they were both pregnant, the court ordered that "the said sentence

Calico Jack was hung on November 18, 1720, and his body was left hanging in public as a warning to others thinking of following his path.

should be respited" and an inspection made. The examination proved they were pregnant and both were reprieved.

Mary Read, spared from execution, contracted fever and died in prison before the birth of her baby. The Parish Register for the district of St. Catherine in Jamaica recorded her burial on April 28, 1721. According to the records, Anne escaped the hangman's noose. What happened to Anne Bonny or her child remains a mystery.

The Golden Age of Piracy ended a few years after the hanging of Calico Jack Rackam and his crew. After 1725, the threat of piracy in the Caribbean declined. But worldwide, piracy was far from annihilated.

Rachel Wall
Boston Pirate

The story of Rachel Wall, an American woman convicted and hanged on Boston Common in 1789, is an example of the small-scale piracy that erupted in the years following the Revolutionary War.

Rachel Wall was born in Carlisle, Pennsylvania, in 1760—the year that brought an end to the French and Indian War. England's victory added to her already vast empire. Canada became English, and England's border now extended all the way to the Mississippi River.

The British Empire's most prized possession remained the thirteen colonies, but the land of "health, plenty and contentment" began to change after the French and Indian War. After George III became king at twenty-two, friction developed as the mother country sought ways to impose taxes on the colonies to help pay England's large war debt.

Although settlers had cleared land for nearly two centuries, America remained a wilderness broken by patches of settlement. A few large cities clustered around the most promising harbors. Towns were small and located great distances apart. Nine out of ten Americans lived off the land.

Rachel Wall's father was a farmer. Growing up on a farm meant hard work for the entire family. Rachel, her three brothers, and two sisters put in long days laboring in the fields. Then there were the daily chores: milking cows, feeding the farm animals, and gathering eggs.

Rachel described her parents as "honest and reputable." She credited them with giving her a good education and instructing her in the fundamental principles of Christianity. "They . . . taught me the fear of God, and if I had followed the good advice and pious counsel they often gave me, I should never have come to this untimely fate," she remembered.

Her devout father offered family prayers in his house every morning and evening. On Sunday night, he gathered his family and read from the Bible, pausing to test the children on the passages.

The signing of the Declaration of Independence took place when Rachel was sixteen. The war brought additional hardships to the rugged farm life and the dull, dusty village of Carlisle.

At a young age, Rachel left home without her parents' consent. She returned again and "was received by them, but could not be contented; therefore I tarried with them but two years before I left them again, and I have never seen them since."

She ran away to Philadelphia with sailor George Wall,

to whom she was "lawfully married." They remained there for some time. George, too, had a restless and discontented nature. Leaving Philadelphia, they traveled to New York. Three months later, the Walls headed to Boston.

Soon George went to sea on a fishing schooner, leaving Rachel. With George away, Rachel worked as a servant in a fine house in Boston and "lived very contented."

Two months later, George returned. Rachel reported that "as soon as he came back, he enticed me to leave my service and take to bad company, from which I may date my ruin." Besides her husband, the bad company included George's five shipmates and their rowdy female companions. The sailors spent their earnings in less than a week. One night while George and his friends were out late carousing, the fishing schooner sailed without them.

With no prospects for making money, George suggested to his companions that they become pirates and get rich. During the Revolutionary War, all the men had served aboard privateers, capturing British ships, plundering them, and dividing the spoils with the government as part of the war effort.

George Wall and his cronies knew that piracy in peacetime was a hanging offense. Still, they were unable to resist the temptation of a life of luxury. The sailors agreed with George's plan. Even Rachel accepted the invitation.

Wall had his pirate crew but no ship. An acquaintance owned a fast fishing schooner, but no longer fished because he was an invalid. George persuaded the man to let him borrow the idle schooner, promising him a share of the catch. The crew fished during good weather, selling their catch at Plymouth Harbor. But the first time a storm came up, Wall put his scheme into action.

George scudded into a small, secluded harbor at the Isles of Shoals and moored the schooner to ride out the gale. As the winds subsided, the captain ordered his crew to hoist sail and put out to sea.

When they reached the busy shipping lanes, Wall shouted to his crew to seize the sails, pull them loose, and twist them for a storm-battered look. Then he hoisted the distress signal. Rachel, dressed in tattered female clothing, was the bait. She stood on deck, pretending to be a pathetic survivor on the hulk. With Rachel's thirst for excitement, it is not hard to imagine her playing the role to the hilt.

The wait was not long. Rachel waved her arms for help as a fishing schooner from Plymouth drew alongside. Only four men were aboard her. The captain, seeing Rachel and the sails torn and hanging slack, offered passage into port to Captain Wall, his wife, and his five-man crew. The disguise worked.

Once on board the schooner, George gave the signal. He and his men drew their knives and slit the throats of the fishermen. Working on the decks, slippery with blood, the murderers tied weights to the bodies and threw them overboard.

Boston Harbor as it looked during the short life of Rachel Wall.

From this escapade, the pirates gained $360 in cash, some expensive fishing gear and several hundred pounds of fish ready for market. They transferred the booty from the Plymouth schooner to the borrowed schooner. The crew scuttled the boat. Nothing remained as the waves washed over the last of the sinking ship.

The pirates returned to the Isles of Shoals. A few days later, they went into Plymouth to sell the stolen fishing gear. They explained that it had washed up on the shore after the big storm.

Five weeks later, a hurricane struck the New England coast. Captain Wall and his crew set out to sea in the storm's wake. They sighted a trading vessel. Rachel donned her tattered clothes again and stood at the rail, waving frantically for help.

The rescue ship was a sloop from Penobscot with a crew of seven. Instead of accepting their kind offer to come aboard, Wall shouted to the captain that he wanted to stay with his ship and try to make repairs. He invited the captain and mate to come aboard to help stop a leak. The two men descended into the hold. Wall and one of his crew thrust a knife into each man's back.

Going above deck, George called to the other vessel that their captain needed some wedges. Two sailors brought the wedges over and took them below. They were killed. The three remaining seamen met similar deaths. Seven murders produced a profit of $550 from the captain's chest and $870 from merchandise.

The Walls continued to prey on vessels into the next year. The raids provided a steady income—though by no means the wealth they had anticipated. George seemed to have an uncanny sense of the moment when a storm had subsided—the right moment to set sail.

One summer day, anchored at their usual spot off the Isles of Shoals, they waited for a hurricane to pass. The sun came out briefly. Captain Wall ordered his men to set sail.

They reached open sea as the howling wind and rain returned in all their fury. What Wall had assumed to be the end of the storm was the calm at the eye of the hurricane. For the first time, he had misjudged the whimsical nature of a storm. Rain pelted the crew as they tried to adjust the sails. Mountainous waves cascaded over the bow, causing the fishing schooner to buck and toss like a giant seesaw. Then a sound like the boom of a cannon pierced the air.

Terrified, Rachel watched as the mainmast snapped in two. George clung to the rigging with one hand, but the crewman beside him was swept overboard by the sheer force of the surging waves. As the storm intensified, the waves increased in size. One mighty billow enveloped George, wresting his hand loose and pushing him over the rail into the yawning dark chasm.

The next day, a brig from New York rescued the survivors. For the first time, Rachel Wall's distress was sincere.

That marked the end of piracy for Rachel Wall.

The ship dropped her off at Boston, where she returned to her old job as a servant in Beacon Hill. But she could not stop lying and stealing. Money and valuables were kept on the ships docked in Boston harbor. For her, the risk of being apprehended increased the excitement. Knowing the places where men hid money and valuables had become second nature to Rachel during her days of piracy.

She formed the habit of slipping down to the waterfront late at night and boarding ships. A good place to search for valuables was the captain's head—the latrine reserved for the exclusive use of the master of the ship. In the spring of 1787, she went aboard a ship lying at the Long Wharf in Boston. She recollected that "on my entering the cabin, the door of which not being fastened, and finding the Captain and Mate asleep in their beds, I hunted about for plunder, and discovered under the Captain's head, a black silk handkerchief containing upwards of thirty pounds in gold crowns and small change, on which I immediately seized the booty and decamped therewith as quick as possible, which money I spent freely . . . full proving the old adage, 'Light come, light go.'"

On another occasion, Rachel broke into a sloop, anchored at Doane's Wharf. She found the captain and every hand on board asleep. "I looked round to see what I could help myself to, when I spied a silver watch hanging over the Captain's head, which I pocketed. I also took a pair of

A woodcut depicting the execution of Rachel Wall, the last woman hung in Boston Common.

silver buckles out of the Captain's shoes: I likewise made free with a parcel of small change for pocket money, to make myself merry among my evil companions and made my escape without being discovered."

Rachel even confessed to a robbery that another poor wretch was supposed to have committed. "I . . . declare Miss Dorothy Horn, a crippled person in Boston Alms House, to be entirely innocent of the theft at Mr. Vaughn's in Essex-Street, tho' she suffered a long imprisonment, was set on the gallows one hour and whipped five stripes therefor."

If one believes this light-fingered woman's dying confession, she was never caught at any of the crimes she committed, and she did not commit the offense for which she was charged.

According to her story, on her way home one evening after work, "without design to injure any person," she heard a noise in the street. She was quite surprised "when the crime was laid to my charge."

Details of the incident are sketchy. With Rachel's penchant for pilfering, it is easy to imagine that she could not control the overpowering urge to snatch the fancy bonnet off the head of an expensively dressed young girl walking toward her. Striking the young woman to the ground, she jammed the girl's bonnet on her own head and fled. She clung to the bonnet as it flapped in the wind. But she was unable to outrun the pursuing officer.

Rachel Wall was tried on September 10, 1789. The

charge delivered to the jury was that "she feloniously did assault and take from the person of Margaret Bender, one bonnet of the value of seven shillings."

Although she admitted on the witness stand to being a pirate and a thief, she insisted that in her pirate days she never murdered anyone. She protested her innocence of the robbery charge to the last. The verdict handed down was that she be returned to jail to await execution. There was no appeal from a defense counsel, no public protest, nor any request for a stay of execution.

On the day of the hanging, October 7, 1789, the maple trees encircling Boston Common were a riot of color. A crowd gathered early. According to the spectators, Rachel's face appeared to be carved in stone. She chose not to say any last words. Maybe she was thinking of the last words of the confession she had made a few hours earlier: "And now into the hands of Almighty God I commit my soul, relying on his mercy, through the merits and meditations of my Redeemer, and die an unworthy member of the Presbyterian Church in the 29th year of my age."

Pirate Rachel Wall was the last woman hanged in Boston Common.

Fanny Campbell
Revolutionary Pirate

Suppose someone said to you: "I possess knowledge concerning your ancestors which you might not wish to discover. If you so desire, I will share this knowledge. If not, the information dies with me." How would you respond?

In 1917, Dr. Charles Edward Lovell posed this question to a relative, John Austin Belden of Wareham, Massachusetts. Unable to contain his curiosity, John said, "Come on, Charles, let's have it."

Dr. Lovell disclosed that one of Belden's ancestors had turned pirate over a hundred years before and was never apprehended. He explained that the entire story, written in a pamphlet, was in his possession—and if John Belden would like to know its contents, he would will it to him.

Following Dr. Lovell's death in October 1930, John Belden received the document with its startling revelation. Belden hastened upstairs. There he opened the envelope that contained not only the astounding history of Fanny Campbell, his great-great-grandmother, but also a drawing of her in color. He stayed in his room until the remarkable story of his ancestor unfolded before his eyes.

The Lovell family lived next to the Campbells at the base of High Rock, in Lynn, Massachusetts, north of Boston. As Fanny matured, she fell in love with William Lovell, who was a year older. William loved Fanny, although she wasn't like most girls. Fanny rode horses and was a sharpshooter who killer panthers in Lynn Woods. She knew all about sailing and could handle a sailboat as well as any man.

Fanny Campbell was eighteen, William nineteen, when what later became known as the "Boston Tea Party" took place. On Monday, December 20, 1773, the *Boston Gazette* reported: "A number of brave & resolute men . . . emptied every chest of tea on board. . . amounting to 342 chests into the sea!" King George III imposed further restrictions on the colony of Massachusetts.

About this time, William Lovell, who enjoyed sailing and fishing, decided to become a deep-sea sailor. For six months, he sailed aboard a New England merchant ship and returned tanned and mature. The changes in her young friend, and William's exciting tales of visits to foreign lands, fascinated Fanny. She confided to William that she, too, yearned to make an ocean voyage.

On the eve of his second sailing, the two young lovers climbed to the top of High Rock. They talked of the future. William explained that although he had a chance to sail aboard the *Royal Kent* bound for South America and the

Indies, he would leave the sea if she wished. Fanny urged him to work until he was captain of his own ship.

William Lovell sailed the next day. He was away for two years. During that time, Fanny had another caller. Captain Robert Burnet was an officer in the British Navy, assigned to a British warship anchored in Boston harbor. At first, Captain Burnet showed casual interest in Fanny. Later, his attentiveness turned to love. But Fanny waited for William. Far at sea, William thought of the girl back in Lynn and determined to marry her on his return voyage.

When a pirate schooner displaying skull and crossbones loomed on the horizon, the captain of William's ship ordered all hands to prepare the cannons for defense. BOOM! BOOM! BOOM! The six-pounders caused damage to the sea ruffians. But they continued to come nearer and nearer. The bearded, sunburned pirates, armed with cutlasses and pistols, threw grapnels—a type of hook—across to the *Royal Kent* and boarded her. In a short time, the sea bandits overwhelmed the American sailors.

In the skirmish, the captain of the *Royal Kent* killed the pirate leader. Moments later, one of the pirates ran a sword through the American captain. The sailors killed more than twice the number they lost but could not hold the ship. The remaining pirates forced the American survivors to join their ranks. The pirates then scuttled the *Royal Kent.*

Lovell, seriously wounded in the battle, watched as the

Royal Kent sank to the bottom of the ocean. After his recovery, he assumed an active role in sailing the pirate craft.

The pirates went ashore at Tortuga Island in the Caribbean. Each man buried his share of the loot taken from the *Royal Kent,* supposedly, in a secret hiding place away from his fellow pirates.

Soon after, the pirates went to sea again. They headed toward Cuba, but before reaching the shores of Cuba, the wind died. Their craft lay becalmed. Lovell and two companions, Jack Herbert and Henry Breed, were on the graveyard watch.

The three New Englanders decided to make a break before morning. They headed the schooner into the light wind that had sprung up and tied the wheel so the ship would stay on course. Slipping a small boat over the side, they lowered a few provisions and scrambled down a rope ladder into the dinghy.

The sailors rowed desperately until they were out of range of the pirates. When the breeze freshened, they hoisted sail for Havana. Eventually, the dirty and ragged sailors, elated by their escape from the pirates, reached the Cuban capital.

Their joy was short-lived. Cuban officials arrested the three Americans on suspicion of being pirates and threw them into jail because they had no proof of being forced aboard the pirate ship. They waited week after week for their trial. Six months passed before they appeared in court where, with no evidence against them, the judge returned them to their cells.

Back in Massachusetts, Fanny Campbell longed for word from William. Months went by. Captain Burnet continued his visits. Fanny remained true to William.

In Havana, two years after the imprisonment, William's friend, Jack Herbert, escaped and made his way to an American ship at the pier. After telling his story, he received permission to hide aboard the vessel and sail back to Boston.

Shortly after landing, Jack Herbert delivered a dirty, crumpled letter to Fanny from William. Clutching the unexpected letter, Fanny questioned Jack about the Cuban prison. He described the prison as heavily guarded.

Before Herbert left, she obtained his address. Fanny Campbell told him to be ready at a moment's notice for a strange adventure that might take place at any time, day or night. Although mystified by her secretive manner, Jack Herbert agreed.

The following evening, Captain Burnet called on Fanny and learned that William was still alive. Fanny convinced Burnet that William was the one for her. His hopes dashed, the disappointed captain left.

One week later, a man dressed as a sailor knocked on Jack Herbert's door and reminded him of his promise to Fanny Campbell. Following instructions, Herbert, posing as a common sailor, went aboard the heavily armed *Constance*, anchored in Boston Harbor. She was set to sail for England by way of Cuba.

The captain of the *Constance* was a tyrant named Brownless. The first mate, Banning, was a dimwit. The second officer was an unusual character named Channing, who had joined the crew the day before. The men admired him for his ease on board ship. Channing knew something the crew didn't. Captain Brownless planned to press the entire crew into the British navy once they reached England. Channing decided to use the captain's scheme to his advantage.

When the *Constance* was about a day's sail from Cuba, Channing went to the captain's cabin. Seizing a brace of pistols from the captain's table and a cutlass from the bulkhead, Channing confronted the captain.

"Captain Brownless, you are my prisoner!"

The captain muttered, "Mutiny!" With his weapons gone, however, he had little choice. Channing tied up the captain, locked him in his quarters, and ordered Jack Herbert to call the crew aft.

With the crew assembled on deck, Channing explained the captain's devious plot to press every sailor into the British navy. The men cheered their acceptance of Channing as the new captain.

All was not well, however. The ship's British cook made plans to kill Channing. Meanwhile, Brownless managed to escape his cabin, intent on the same bloody errand. The two men met in the darkness outside the entrance to Channing's quarters and, mistaking each other for Channing, they engaged in deadly combat. The following morning, a crew member stumbled upon their bodies. The remains of the two men were dropped over the side of the ship.

The *Constance*, now a pirate craft with Channing as captain, overpowered a British bark, the *George*. Jack Herbert commanded the new ship.

A few days later, as the ships sailed side by side, mutiny broke out aboard the *George*. Captain Channing watched from the other craft as Herbert was roped and thrown on the deck. Crossing over at once in a small boat, Channing boarded the vessel with drawn pistols, killed one of the mutineers, and put an end to the mutiny.

Late one night, the two ships sailed into Havana Bay. Channing ordered Jack Herbert to pick eight loyal crew members and tell them about the fort where Lovell and Breed were prisoners.

Herbert and eight sailors rowed to the fort. Leaving a man to guard the rowboat, the others slithered along the sandy beach. They sighted a mute form ahead. A Spanish sentry! Sneaking to the rear of the guard, a sailor silenced forever the unfortunate Spaniard. Three more sentries met the same fate. The sailors locked the four bodies in the guardhouse.

They crept into the subterranean passageway leading to the cell. Using keys taken from the guards, Herbert unlocked the cell door and awakened Lovell and Breed. They

Fanny Campbell, disguised as a man, sailed into Havana, Cuba, to rescue her future husband.

sprinted out of the jail. An hour later, all eleven Americans were in the small boat, rowing desperately for the brig. Just as the two vessels set sail, they heard the unmistakable roll of the fort drums signaling the discovery of the daring feat. But it was too late. The American ships sailed away from shore and out of danger from the Spaniards.

Channing appointed William Lovell first mate of the *Constance*. Several days later, the captain called Lovell to his cabin and revealed to the astonished mate that Captain Channing was in reality Fanny Campbell. Fanny's disguise—skin dyed brown, hair cropped short, and wearing a marine officer's uniform—served her well. Even William failed to recognize her! Fanny cautioned William against letting the crew know.

The *Constance* and the *George* continued their voyage uneventfully until they met and seized a British merchant ship. They learned from the crew that the Revolutionary War was in full swing. To escape the stigma of piracy, Fanny persuaded the sailors to give up their pirating ways and turn privateer. Now, instead of robbing any ship that came along for their own profit, the crew of the two crafts would work for the American government, capturing only enemy ships and turning a share of the booty over the Continental Congress.

Soon, the *Constance* and the *George* captured a British armed sloop. It was quite a shock to Fanny when the captain of the sloop turned out to be her former suitor, Captain Burnet. He was shackled below deck along with the other prisoners. Although Captain Burnet recognized Fanny, he did not reveal her identity.

When Fanny learned from the prisoners that the British now occupied Boston, she set a course for Marblehead. A week later, the crews of the *Constance* and the *George* became legal privateers of the new nation. They received "letters of marque," or commissions—carrying on the centuries old tradition of allowing citizens to attack and plunder enemy ships during wartime.

During the Revolution, Congress issued 1,700 letters of marque and reprisal. The Atlantic coast, with its hundreds of bays and inlets and scores of rivers emptying into the ocean, was ideal for privateering. Not only did the British blockade stop American trade; it threw thousands of sailors out of work.

Sailors signed aboard a privateer out of a mixture of anger, need, and greed. They made more than a thousand dollars in just one British prize at a time when families lived comfortably on nine dollars a month.

For all of its promise of wealth, privateering was risky. British warships captured hordes of American privateers. Because they were not in the armed forces, they were not considered prisoners of war. In British eyes, they were pirates who could not be hanged for fear of reprisal. The British solved the problem by keeping them under conditions in which many would die anyhow. They converted large old warships into hulks or floating dungeons. The hulks, stripped of sails and fittings and boarded up port-holes, kept the prisoners completely sealed in except for small slits cut in the ships' sides for air. When they had food, it was spoiled and crawled with insects. According to a prisoner who survived, the water was "an astonishing greenish-yellow that had a foul, sour smell."

Over thirteen thousand Americans—more than the total killed in George Washington's army—died of disease and starvation aboard the filthy, rat-infested floating prisons. Privateers who avoided the hulks captured and brought in over three thousand British ships, most of them merchant vessels.

Before heading back to sea as a privateer, William married Fanny. As far as we know, Fanny never went to sea again.

William served his country as a privateer until the war ended. Later, he made several long trips to China and then retired from the sea.

William and Fanny Lovell had a large family. Apparently, at the time their sons and daughters were growing up, it was common knowledge that Fanny turned pirate to rescue her loved one.

Cheng I Sao
Chinese Pirate and Warlord

After piracy had virtually ceased elsewhere in the world, it flourished in the South China Sea. Piracy was by no means new to this region. Its beginnings date back to the fourth century B.C. But famine, overpopulation, increased maritime trade, and weak government accounted for the rise in piracy in the early 1800s.

Bloodthirsty sailors roamed the rivers and coastal waters in junks—flat-bottomed boats designed for speed and navigation in shallow waters. In 1809, a Chinese admiral complained: "The pirates are too powerful, we cannot master them by our arms . . ."

The most powerful pirate of all was a woman, Cheng I Sao (1775-1844). At one time, she commanded a fleet of 2000 junks and 70,000 men and women—a force that outnumbered the total number of participants in the Spanish Armada in 1588 by two to one. A Chinese chronicle based on firsthand information of the pirates and their activities was published during Cheng I Sao's lifetime. Also, a number of captives recorded for posterity their experiences aboard the pirate ships.

During the first decade of the nineteenth century, the waters around Canton, Macao, and Hong Kong were thick with pirate junks. Piracy was a struggle to survive—with a revolutionary tinge. Hordes of impoverished fishermen locked into recurring cycles of debt and dockworkers unable to make a living joined forces with the pirates, plundering ships and waging war on corrupt Mandarin rule.

Most of the rank and file of the pirates must have seen piracy as a means to trade their drab existence on shore for a life of adventure. Many were driven by the desire to escape the tyranny of officials and taxes. However, the majority who turned to piracy went in search of profits.

As wives of the men, women participated fully in piracy. Most of the propelling and sculling of the lighter vessels was regarded as women's work. They also took part in combat.

In 1801, Cheng I Sao married into the Cheng family, which had been involved in piracy since the late seventeenth century. The story is told that her husband, the pirate leader Cheng I, a hunchback and son of a peasant, was forced to go to sea because his father couldn't afford to feed him. He turned pirate and engaged in sporadic attacks on ocean-going traders. Cheng I's sea robbers made raids inland, including slaves in their booty.

When the time came that Cheng I was ready to take a wife, twenty captured females, bound hand and foot, were

Cheng I Sao and her organization were pirates in the South China sea, off the coast of Hong Kong.

brought before him. One of the women was Hsi Kai, a graceful peasant girl, with skin "of the tint of rich cream but at the cheek became a deep rose. Her eyes were black and would shine like jet, and the same black sheen was in her hair." It is said that "before the beauty of her face, the eyes of men grew confused."

Dazzled by this stunning creature, Cheng I had her untied. Her feet were not deformed by binding, as prescribed by Chinese custom. The moment she was set free, Hsi Kai lunged at the fat old pirate chief, almost scratching his eyes out before being pulled away. Despite her aggressive temperament, Cheng I offered her jewels, cosmetics, brightly colored silks, and slaves if she would consent to be his wife.

In a bold move for a Chinese woman, she demanded—and got—a full half share of his wealth, in addition to joint command of his pirate fleet.

The story may or may not be true, but Cheng I and his wife emerged as leaders of a successful pirate confederation composed of six principal fleets.

Cheng I Sao—her name means "wife of Cheng I"—assisted her husband in the creation of the confederation. Colored banners of red, yellow, blue, green, black, and white distinguished the Chengs' fleets.

As a squadron commander, Cheng I Sao demonstrated skill, cunning, and leadership. Her strategy was to take the enemy by surprise and overpower them in hand-to-hand

The Chinese pirate junk was the ship used to terrorize shipping in the South China sea.

combat. She usually concealed most of their vessels behind a promontory—a long strip of land jutting into the sea—and sent out two or three as decoys. After the initial contact with a likely target, the remaining ships surrounded the boat.

The most lethal weapons were bamboo pikes with sharp, saber-like blades of varying lengths. Fire was another weapon. Large boats filled with straw were set ablaze. The winds tormented the flames to fury as these floating fireballs made their way into the fleets of their adversaries. They hurled smaller firebrands out of long hollow bamboos, aimed at enemy sails.

At times, the pirates went into battle with faces aflame and eyes aglow as a result of drinking a mixture of wine and gunpowder. To bolster their courage, they sometimes ate the hearts of vanquished foes. In combat, they repeatedly sprinkled themselves with garlic water as a charm to ward off bullets.

The pirates preferred to operate in the less treacherous coastal waters. They plundered villages, markets, and rice fields on shore, assisted by local bandits. By late 1805, pirate-bandit raids occurred regularly.

On December 7, 1806, John Turner, chief mate of the *Tay*, was captured by Cheng I. He was held for ransom for five months and wrote an account of his captivity. He estimated Chengs' fleet as between five and six hundred vessels divided into six squadrons. Each operated in its own allotted area of the China coast. In major expeditions, the squadrons banded together. The bigger junks carried twelve guns as well as rowboats armed with swivel guns.

Turner's food consisted of skimpy portions of coarse red rice and occasionally some salt fish. He described the conditions on board ship as "wretched" and related that: "At night the space allowed me to sleep in was never more than about eighteen inches wide, and four feet long; and if at any time I happened to extend my contracted limbs beyond their limits, I was sure to be reminded of my mistake by a blow or kick."

Before his release in 1807, John Turner suffered cruel treatment and witnessed some gruesome scenes. He described the fate of a Chinese naval officer: "I saw one man . . . nailed to the deck through his feet with large nails, then beaten with four rattans twisted together, till he vomited blood; and after remaining some time in this state, he was taken ashore and cut to pieces."

"On the seventeenth day of the tenth month in the twentieth year of Kea king," (November 1807), Cheng I Sao's husband "perished in a heavy gale."

Following the unexpected death of Cheng I, the Chinese pirates gathered to elect a new leader. One story described the meeting. Cheng I Sao attended, dressed in the chief's uniform: "embroidered dragons writhed over" the robe of purple, blue, red, and gold. In her sash, she wore "some of her dead husband's swords." On her head was "his familiar war helmet."

"Look at me, captains," she said to the assembled group. "Your departed chief sat in council with me. Your most powerful fleet, the White, under my command, took more prizes than any other did. Do you think I will bow to any other chief?"

And so Cheng I Sao, instead of retiring to chaste widowhood, became head of the pirate hierarchy.

In her first act as chief, she appointed twenty-one-year-old Chang Pao, her "adopted" son, as commander of the Red Flag fleet. Chang Pao, (also referred to as Paou) a fisherman's son, had joined the pirates at age fifteen after being captured by Cheng I, who "liked him so much, that he could not depart from him" and eventually made him commander of a ship. In time, Chang Pao became the lover and later the husband of Cheng I Sao.

Cheng I Sao ruled her fleet with a hand of iron. She required her men to adhere to a code of conduct that regulated all aspects of their life. This "code of law" was harsh and kept the men united and well disciplined. Any seaman who went ashore without permission would have his ears slit; a repetition of the same unlawful act meant death. Mistreatment of a woman prisoner resulted in execution. Stealing from village suppliers and pilfering from the common treasury were also capital offenses.

All loot was entered on the warehouse register. Cheng I Sao operated on such a large scale that, unlike the usual practice of pirates, she required written records. Any pirate wishing to draw from the common fund made a written application to the secretary of the storehouse, who was called the Ink and Writing Master. Cheng I Sao referred to the plundering of a ship as "trans-shipping of goods."

Like the other boat dwellers of the South China Sea, the pirates prayed to their gods before each foray. If reports from the gods were unfavorable, they would not undertake a mission. The flamboyant Chang Pao, who usually dressed in a purple silk robe and a black turban, had a magnificent temple constructed aboard his largest ship.

Under the pirate confederation, captives were a significant source of manpower. One government official estimated that captives made up more than half of the entire force, most of who served the pirates without any chance of release.

The Chinese pirates captured Richard Glasspoole, an officer on the East India Company ship, Marquis of Ely, and seven British seafarers on September 21, 1809. Until his release on December 7, Glasspoole kept a diary of life on board a pirate junk.

Glasspoole wrote that the pirates "have no settled residence on shore, but live constantly in their vessels." Every man was allowed "a small berth about four feet square," to stow his wife and family. "From the number of souls crowded in so small a space," he reported, "it must naturally be supposed they are horribly dirty, which is evidently the case, and their vessels swarm with all kinds of vermin."

According to Glasspoole, certain species of rats, encouraged to breed, were eaten as "great delicacies." He noted there were "very few creatures" they would not eat. "During our captivity we lived three weeks on caterpillars boiled with rice!"

Glasspoole's account describes the pirates as being "much addicted to gambling." Their leisure hours were spent "at cards and smoking opium."

Glasspoole and his men witnessed entire villages being destroyed and men, women, and children massacred. The Englishmen were forced to participate in the carnage.

A Chinese historian describes a battle between the pirates and the villagers of Kan-shih. As the pirates made their way into the village, one hundred women hid in the surrounding paddy fields. "The pirates on hearing a child crying" captured the women and children. One of the women, Mei Ying, "was very beautiful, and a pirate being about to seize her by the head, she abused him exceedingly." In the skirmish, "the pirate dragged her down and broke two of her teeth, which filled her mouth and jaws with blood." As the pirate approached her again, "she laid hold of his garments with her bleeding mouth and threw both him and herself into the river where they were drowned."

Cheng I Sao's financial operation included a protection racket whereby she sold "safe passage" protection on land as well as sea. During September 1809, Richard Glasspoole accompanied the pirates on one of their fee-collecting

This illustration of Cheng I Sao in action was drawn during her life.

missions. Five hundred junks sailed up the Pearl River. Glasspoole's boat anchored close to a village. The crews burned the customs house and readied their rowboats for attack.

A messenger went into the village and demanded a payment of ten thousand dollars annually. When payment was refused, the pirates threatened to destroy the town and murder all the inhabitants. The two sides finally agreed on a "fee" of six thousand dollars, "which they were to collect by the time of our return down the river," said Glasspoole.

On October 1, 1809, Glasspoole witnessed the capture of two hundred fifty women and children. It was a "melancholy sight to see women in tears, clasping their infants in their arms and imploring mercy for them from those brutal robbers . . . They were unable to escape with the men owing to that abominable practice of cramping their feet. . . . In fact, they might all be said to totter, rather than walk." He notes that "twenty of the female captives were brought on board the ship on which I was." They were hauled on board by the hair and treated in a most savage manner. Several of the women "leaped over-board and drowned themselves," rather than submit to the horrific abuse.

One of Glasspoole's sailors was rounding a corner during a skirmish when he met a pirate with a "drawn sword in his hand" and "two Chinamen's heads" tied by their pigtails slung around his neck. He was chasing a third victim. On this occasion, Chang Pao had offered ten dollars for every head produced.

Finally, Richard Glasspoole and his men were ransomed for a handsome sum and delivered from "a miserable captivity, which we had endured for eleven weeks and three days."

At the time of Glasspoole's liberation, the confederation was at the height of its power. Yet the association survived only a few months longer. Dissension broke out among the pirates. Then, in a complete turnabout, the Chinese emperor, unable to conquer the pirates, offered amnesty. Like the European rulers, the settlement included a pardon, money, and land to any pirate who would surrender.

Cheng I Sao understood the advantages of the offer. On April 18, 1810, leading a delegation of seventeen women and children, she went unarmed to the governor-general in Canton to negotiate. Two days later the surrender took place.

Throughout her years as a pirate, Cheng I Sao acted in open defiance of Confucian customs. She expanded the pirate empire after Cheng I's death. The confederation prospered as she won the support of her followers, issued orders, planned military campaigns, and exercised her business acumen.

In less than a decade after the dismantling of the confederation, Chang Pao rose to the post of colonel in the military bureaucracy. Cheng I Sao made this high position possible.

He died at the age of thirty-six, ending the spectacular rise of this illiterate fisherman's son.

Cheng I Sao, widowed a second time, spent her last days in Canton, "leading a peaceful life so far as consistent with the keeping of an infamous gambling house." The Chinese dragon lady died in 1844 at the age of sixty-nine.

Though the days of the great commanders like Cheng I Sao were over, the tradition of piracy never died out entirely in the South China seas. Pirate raids continued, but they were considerably curbed by the introduction of steam power in the nineteenth century. Pirates, relying on the wind to sail, were easily trapped by the steamers that could sail anywhere, even on a windless day.

China's growing economy has spawned a new wave of sophisticated sea piracy in the late twentieth century. The new sea wolves run organized criminal syndicates, making tens of thousands of dollars a year from what are known as "phantom ships" with fake names. The booty are no longer spices, silks, and gold, but easily disposable goods such as electronics and cash. Ships are hijacked and, once out at sea, repainted, renamed, and the illegal cargo sold.

The swashbuckling days of men—and women—pirates remain a haunting shadow of the past. But as long as the lure of easy money and sheer adventure on the high seas exists, piracy in some fashion may never be completely eradicated from the maritime world.

Bibliography

American Heritage. *Pirates of the Spanish Main*. New York: American Heritage Publishing Co., Inc., 1961.

Botting, Douglas. *The Pirates*. New York: Time-Life Books, Inc., 1978.

Brooke, Henry K. *Book of Pirates*. Philadelphia: J.B. Perry, 1847.

Chambers, Anne. *Granuaile: The Life and Times of Grace O'Malley*. Dublin, Ireland: Wolfhound Press, 1994.

Ellms, Charles. *The Pirates Own Book*. Salem, MA: Marine Research Society, 1924.

Elton, Oliver.(translator). *The First Nine Books of the Danish History of Grammaticus*. David Nutt, 1894.

Foster, R. F.(ed). *The Oxford Illustrated History of Ireland*. Oxford: Oxford University Press, 1989.

Glasspoole, Richard. *Mr. Glasspoole and the Chinese Pirates*. London: Golden Cockerel Press, 1935.

Gollomb, Joseph. *Pirates Old and New*. New York: The Macaulay Company, 1928.

Gosse, Philip. *The History of Piracy*. (First published in 1932). Glorieta, NM: The Rio Grande Press, Inc., 1990.

Johnson, Captain Charles. *A General History of the Robberies and Murders of the most Notorious Pyrates* (1724). Published as Daniel Defoe *A General History of the Pyrates*, Manuel Schonhorn (ed.). Columbia, SC: University of South Carolina Press, 1972.

Keller, Allan. *Colonial America*. New York: Hawthorn Books, 1971.

"Life, Last Words and Dying Confession of Rachel Wall," Boston Goal, October 7, 1789. Evans Early American Imprint microcard series, No. 22235. Columbia, SC: University of South Carolina.

Manthorpe, Jonathan. "Asian Gangs Use 'Phantom Ships' to Steal Cargo: Growing Economy in China Fuels Sophisticated Sea Piracy by Organized Crime," *Vancouver Sun* (Vancouver, B.C.), May 4, 1995, A 22.

Matthew, David. "Cornish and Welsh Pirates in the Reign of Elizabeth," *English Historical Review*, July 1924, Vol. No. XXXIX.

Marx, Jennifer. *Pirates and Privateers of the Carribean*. Malabar, FL: Krieger Publishing Company, 1992.

Mitchell, David J. *Pirates*. London: Thames & Hudson Ltd., 1976.

Murray, Dian H. *Pirates of the South China Coast 1790-1810*. Stanford, CA: Stanford University Press, 1987.

Neumann, Charles Fried. (translator). *History of the Pirates Who Infested The China Sea from 1807 to 1810*. Translation of Yuen Yunglun, *Ching hai-fen chi*. London, 1831.

O'Brien, William. *A Queen of Men*. London: T. Fisher Unwin, 1898.

Poertner, Rudolf. *The Vikings*. Translated by Sophie Wilkins. London, St. James Press, 1971.

Pringle, Patrick. *Jolly Roger: The Story of the Great Age of Piracy*. New York: W.W. Norton, Inc., 1953.

Sherry, Frank. *Raiders and Rebels*. New York: Hearst Marine Books, 1986.

Smith-Lucie, Edward. *Outcasts of the Sea*. New York: Paddington Press LTD, 1978.

Snow, Edward Rowe. *True Tales of Pirates and Their Gold*. New York: Dodd, Mead & Company, 1966.

Stanley, Jo (ed.). *Bold in Her Breeches: Women Pirates Across the Ages*. London: Pandora, 1995.

Stewart, Gail B. *The Revolutionary War*. San Diego, CA: Lucent Books, 1991.

Index

Alf, 16, 19-20
Alfhild, 10, 12-20

Barnet, Captain Jonathan, 68
Belden, John Austin, 84
Bender, Margaret, 83
Bingham, Richard, 29-30, 32
Blackbeard, 61
Bonny, Anne (Cormac), 45,
    56-62, 64, 66, 68-70, 72
Bonny, James, 60-61
Borgar, 19, 20
Boston Gazette, 85
boucans, 51
Bourke, Richard-in-Iron, 28-29
Bourke, Theobald, 28-30, 33
Breed, Henry, 87, 90
Brennan, Peg, 57
Brownless, Captain, 89-90
buccaneer, 51, 53
Burnet, Captain Robert, 86,
    88, 92-93

Caesar, Julius, 10
Campbell, Fanny, 84-86, 88-94
Chang Pao, 102-103, 107-108

Cheng I, 96, 98, 100-101
Cheng I Sao, 10, 95-98, 101-105,
    107-108

Cobham, Eric, 34-36, 38-40,
    42-44
Cobham, Maria (Lindsey), 34-35,
    38-44
Columbus, Christopher, 51
Constance, 88-90, 92-93
Cormac, William, 57-58, 60

Dillon, Thomas, 70
Drake, Francis, 22, 37
Duc de Chartes, 43

Elizabeth I, 21, 25-26, 30-32

freebooters, 51

General History of the Robberies
    and Murders of the Most
    Notorious Pyrates, The,
    45-46, 69
George, 90, 92-93
Glasspoole, Richard, 103-104,
    106-107

Groa, 20
Gurid, 20

Henry VIII, 21
Herbert, Jack, 87-90
Homer, 10
Horn, Dorothy, 82
Hornigold, Ben, 61

Johnson, Captain Charles, 45, 69

King Sigar, 16, 19
King Siward, 15

Lawes, Sir Nicholas, 57
Lovell, Dr. Charles Edward, 84
Lovell, William, 85-88, 90, 92, 94

Mei Ying, 104

O'Flaherty, Donal, 26-27
O'Flaherty, Murrough, 30
O'Flaherty, Owen, 30
O'Malley, Dudora, 22, 23-24
O'Malley, Grace, 21-33
O'Malley, Margaret, 22-24
Osten, 15

Philip of Spain, 21-22
piratas, 52

Rackam, Jack, 56, 61-64, 66, 68-72
Raleigh, Walter, 22
Read, Mary, 45-50, 52, 54, 56-57, 64-70, 72

Rogers, Woodes, 56, 61
Royal Kent, 86-87

Saxo Grammacticus, 12, 14-16, 18, 20
Shakespeare, William, 22
Sidney, Sir Henry, 29

Tay, 100
Thomas, Dorothy, 70
Turner, John, 100-101

Valhalla, 14
Vane, Charles, 61
Varangers, 14
Vikings, 10, 12-14, 17, 20

Wall, George, 74-76, 78-79
Wall, Rachel, 73-76, 78-83
Wemund, 15

zee rovers, 51